# PRAYER OF THE MINSTREL

## SELECTED POEMS

### KEVIN DAVIDSON

*Beauty awakens the soul to act.*

—*Dante*

ISBN: 978-0-9969986-6-6

Hillside Education
475 Bidwell Hill Road
Lake Ariel, PA 18436

www.hillsideeducation.com

# Contents

# Prayer of the Minstrel

*May I arrive through God's soft voice in me*
*Into heaven's song, singing there above*
*And sing my wayward heart back home to thee*
*Those same notes are sung by the Holiest dove.*

*With an invocation to the burning angel choirs*
*Praying a song before our sacred savior's throne*
*How shall I sing the names of all love's fires*
*With the humblest of voices that is only my own.*

*Bring me patience when I'm empty into the night,*
*Bring me harmony in my soul, beaten by wrongs,*
*Bring me voice when I sing the Divine and the Light,*
*And let me give You the world in my humble songs.*

# BOYHOOD'S LAMENT

*When we were boys, young in our bright days*
*We knew the woods and all the secret ways*
*When myth and fact breathed as one, holy and true*
*Then giants walked and gods hung the silver dew.*

*The world as young as we, was steeped in our tales*
*Of knight and king, and dragons guarded hidden dales.*
*Of Poetry's fountain we drank deep and fresh*
*And to us the world was more spirit than flesh.*

*On shores of islands untouched by any man*
*With nymphs and the kings of old we ran,*
*Our swords in our hands, chivalric vows we'd pledge*
*And fight our foe until death's very edge*

*I am not now old, nor grown wise in age,*
*But virtue's games I've left for molding page.*

# HOPE

*Hope is a little lighted flame*
*Still, when night comes crashing down in shame*
*And there burns bold before that last breaking*
*Of the world, half remembered before night came*
*Glimpsed, gleaming gold fire of shiver, shaking*
*A spark for waning world-light, since world's making.*

*Hope is a brave and reckless cry*
*That knowing death and gallant goes to die.*
*Fearless face that fighting, singing death song,*
*Face that fire that ravage earth and sky*
*And though light fall and darkness long,*
*Hope rise and wind a horn forlorn but strong.*

*Hope is Blood upon a tree*
*And the quiet comfort of low bent knee*
*And a humble prayer whispered in the night;*
*Lonely in the dark descends the answered plea,*
*Meek mind belies steady strength and might*
*Guarding there a veiled yet valiant light.*

# INSCAPE

I have met Him here in the day or dark
Grown with the grass gripping there the soil.
He is here hidden steeped in star spark,
He leaps forth like flame from sky torn toil.
Let all eyes see, ears of heart, all souls hark
He rests, He waits in bowls of green grown broil.

Here this tree He is stressed in, rests in, longs
Dim deepening down well brinking and brim
He babbles and sings strings with stream songs;
Seen in body bound lovely in voices, faces and limb
Stone sings stone-song where His harmony belongs,
Bells flung fell, hung, flower bows to Him.

From mist lift lake wafts up and out wade
In sky-shore cloud, heaven fire ripping forth face
Pressed, pied in the sun's rose flame fade
Like light through a window soul's light place,
He stepped down from dim thunder's roaring raid
Now lays latent as embers of crept cold fire lace.

# APPALACHIA

*A ridge line swathed and tree head swallowed*
*Green band belted, and buckled round a hilly waste*
*By crŏokéd creek and singing streaming hollowed,*
*Where the green smell grows thick to the taste*
*And passing cloud dip drips of holy libation rain*
*Casting life light to ease the dry drought pain.*

*Ivy-wound ways of woods treading quiet, cool,*
*Where light underfoot are soft press of grasses.*
*Shelter shadow bright in the deep world cruel*
*And leaf loam beds remember as thin time passes*
*Sun lifted light through valleys cooling fog fade*
*Faith filled forest of mountains' mounting made.*

*Past the valley's dim deepening comfort call*
*Roll the mountains wreathed in morning mist*
*Hued from green to blue and fade into sky hall*
*Here hiding from the planning progress fist*
*Veiled valleys hiding secret sacred flame*
*Within each that breathes and speaks its name.*

# A RED MORNING

An hour before night releases it's clasp
Before the newborn sun breath gasp
A solitary herald, hidden at his post
Sun-crying thrush in the dark and dark lapse
Cloud crested waves break on sky-coast
Thrush lush song calls up a singing host.

Rising ring one by one to a chorus grow
Praise for the gold gleam of glimpsed glow
A thin line of gold blood draws all the hills
The sun's side pierced and blood light flow
Dripping down in a flash of rippling rills
Light leap above the darkened downs or' spills.

The sun is bleeding at its rising red
But lifting light above earth's bowed head
And new washed the hills are cleansed of stain
For that the birds' singing rings at sun bled
Relieved now is the darkened waiting pain
Lighted world by sun's open valiant vein.

# REVELATION 2:17

*The room is lit within and night outside*
*Slipping shadows, shallow, almost seen*
*Tangled tripping, drifted, darkness tied*
*Remembered dreams sifted from what's been*
*    Plowed, plied and piled against the door*
*    Bolted, bound unknown but by the window*
*    The lighted room within and mantle more*
*    The white written stone above fire's glow*
*In you a stone and mantled flame*
*That lights your room and window pane*
*Written there on every knowing name*
*Window show, mantle name, fire reign*
*    Now I see you through a window darkly*
*    But still flames burn in the darkness starkly.*

# ACADEMIA

Down the dust drawn hall pictures hang
Depicting downcast long looking eyes
In faces that never rise never sang
While the stiff chairs sit circled in lies
That they know, and of their virtues
While all the hall is cast in blacks and blues.

The gold gilded flag of logic's claim
Flies flung above the wild fields
Where beauty's roots grow untamed
And walls of words ring round and shield
The pride of gnostic's nostalgic pen
Writing words never seen again.

And still the dust collects and guides
The ships of thought built on sands
Far from where the currents course glides
Under the flowered trees of truth's lands
Guarded and walled by dark stone
And leaves them protected all alone.

# THE BULL

*Horned king's lowing loud and low*
*Fire breath, rushing, rising from below*
*Darkness of a low earth-shook rumble*
*Heaven fell hellward frantic in the tumble*
*Dropped with Light bearer's stricken stumble*
*Staggered, stripped, ripped from the height*
*Now blowing as at the finger's flame of light.*

*Dark sinews strung bounding round*
*The low thrust shoulder, sin bound*
*Torturer's stung pride ripped red and hung*
*And the guilt banner above the green field flung*
*Showing, flying forth black fire from hell forged lung*
*Earth's scars sliced by heaving hooves stand*
*While the blood-rearing head follows pride's hand.*

*Strike low goring life with a back born blow*
*And staring eyes that darkly gleaming glow*
*Pride humbled, heavy hooved and horned*
*Raging power torn and heaven scorned*
*Tragic prince down thrown and never mourned*
*For death of man are his horns committed*
*But power has he only ever counterfeited.*

# THE SACRED GLEN
## (THE REVERSE SONNET)

A stillful pool that lies so lush, beneath
Where holy corps of whitened birches grow
Cast cool within a cupped clay wreath
Where pagans for their worship used to go
   No breath of world without wound down as breeze
   To touch that font, with unseen singing source
   Too gathered grow those mantled guarding trees
   Untouched by time that winds its wearing course
To see again the gods that once lived there
I wish to God that we'd not gone so blind
Such blinded eyes are more than hearts can bear
And this small glen can man no longer find
   Blind eyes that enlightened cannot see
   beauty that once held our hearts to thee.

# MY FLYING, MY FALLING

*My mind must sway, your sway, a one and, two, three*
*As much as my heart joy cries my heart dies*
*Dropped, a stone in currents yours, it drops from me*
*Yet flying up on gold fletched wings, a fluttering rise*
*Thank God that I should granted be grace to feel*
*The dawning draw of hearts, your eyes in mine*
*That line, the lightest chain that binds your hearts in seal,*
*And falls off tongues of poets, rhyming love and time.*
*This seal of which I sing lies yet unspoken,*
*But promised there, within are vow to give.*
*A ring that seals again another seal unbroken*
*By time or wand'rings's lust for new to live.*
*This seal and vows within I'll make and do.*
*I die yet am renewed, reflected here in you.*

# THE GRASS

Like swords of a green clad army brave
Forged of green gleaming, growing deadly steel
In furnaces of fertile earth, up from grave
On earth they guard and earth low kneel
Lords and captains crowned in green and gold
Flashing forth in a sun flung battle bold.

Yet soft laid like goddess garment cast
Aside by spirits of warm life's spring
Caressing those that dancing past
And lift their little voices below to sing
Washed by wells of heaven's moon at night
Inlaid and worked with gold and morning light.

# DAN BERG'S TEA

*He lifts the cup up to his lips*
*A heated sip over tongue he tips*
*Hoping there for relief of mind*
*And soon he's left class far behind.*

*And now he runs or' fields of green*
*To places that he's never seen*
*To save the maid is now his quest*
*And search her out, not stop or rest.*

*His steed is light upon the reign*
*That rears and stamps and shakes its mane*
*Togeth'r they ride both brave and true*
*With strength this strengthened tea imbue.*

*What strength he has he will not spend*
*In reading books from end to end*
*Instead he dreams and rides and fights*
*Chevalier undaunted by steels' cold bites.*

*Far from rooms where logic grows*
*In verdant valleys where the river flows*
*He stops and there a song does sing*
*And drinks so cool from welling spring.*

*There cares and woes he'll set aside*
*And among the trees he'll there abide*
*To pass the night beneath the moon*
*And rise again, there, just past noon.*

◆❖◆❖◆❖◆❖◆❖◆❖◆❖◆❖◆❖◆❖◆❖◆❖◆

*What makes this dream and truth come true?*
*Is drinking tea what we must do*
*This is no tea he drinks today*
*For whiskey wastes the class away.*

# DRAB TREE

*See sitting there a drab dappled tree*
*By weather wilted, wind wither and twisted*
*Such eyes seen worlds we'll never see*
*In structure low among the wonders listed.*

*Of all things maker made so beauty bright*
*This tree holds no majesty as licking lightning flame*
*This dying tree tread upon by mountain might*
*Yet like this tree is there none the same.*

*Form and structure of each and own*
*Pressed here the clay in soul mold*
*Wrapped round inside branch and bone*
*A grace flame laced like inlaid gold.*

# MY SONG OF SONGS

*Like little jewels are your feet*
*Light in dancing, both fair and fleet*
*Your limbs like the graceful sweep of trees*
*Bending lightly in the gently kissing breeze*
*Like stars, your eyes are little lights*
*Burning blue in the dark, deepening nights*
*Trickling fire, your hair on shoulders falls*
*Brighter than the sacred flame in heaven halls*
*Your lips like beads of sky descending dew*
*That kiss earth's face and make it all anew*
*Like a spire, your neck, below the stars' wheel*
*Yet fairer in its rising, in motion and in feel*
*Cresting waves are your shoulders, rolling silent soft*
*And bear the vessel of my hope aloft*
*Like the land are you of warmest soil*
*The lovely bearer of the fruit of my toil*
*Like a liquor smooth and sweet is your voice*
*And to drink that nectar is my only choice*
*Your breath is a warm, and gentle wind on me*
*That fills my sails and lifts me or' the sea*
*As soft falling rain, your touch on the place below*
*On parched and broken earth it falls and there regrow*
*All these things by your beauty are surpassed*
*And of you will I ever sing, both first and last.*

# Spring, The Bride

*When at the sun begun dawn dappled day*
*And spring's singing love songs strings lifted air*
*My love arise from winter's bed where she lay*
*And casts off the cold of whitened beauty bare*
*Changing diamond jeweled snow cloth clung*
*For the well watered emerald necklace hung.*

*Now lifted lies the flakes of marriage veil*
*To reveal the source of lighted life within*
*As dappled press of bright and pale*
*Soft and course wild release relive begin*
*Breaking sin chain. Sweet breaking waking*
*Love in earthy breast, new washed new making.*

*The mountains shrug off their heavy clouded coats*
*Like the ghost lifted from dead God's gasping mouth*
*Lance light in streaming slipping mantle moats*
*And the voice of the dove is heard from the south*
*Reborn, relive, reflect, relate, rekindle, regrow*
*That living flame rising up among the springing water's*
*flow.*

# GROUNDWARD

*Long darkness stretching down*
*Long silence solemnly bound*
*The warmth of fertile earth below*
*Lost light buried by, underground*
*Sleeps that drift so soft, and slow*
*Sleeps that with heavy darkness grow.*

*Walking down, around the stairs*
*That wind groundward with cares*
*While body spirits homeward send*
*Solemnity and darkness only dead dare*
*With bones that break and bend*
*And lost flame to its cold and end.*

*The virtue lost is virtue gained*
*No longer feel staggered strained*
*Grave death enthrones and dead*
*And flesh is now forever stained*
*And death so sleeps in every bed*
*Heat and cold no different to man's heavy head.*

# Shadow

*I admire my shadow in his height*
*He does not look away from the brightness*
*When all others turn and hide from the light*
*And of me he carries only just a likeness*
*Yet without the faults and defects that I hold*
*And he never wavers, never grows he old.*

*He comes to watch the sun set and reborn*
*And in his darkness the light he knows*
*But by that choice his will never torn*
*His friendship never halts and never grows*
*While at my side he stays and stands*
*There is no shaking in his extended hands.*

*I admire my shadow in his height*
*For he know best of the dark and light.*

# WESTWARD

The world of the western sun
Light of the darkening earth
Height of dust's rising rebirth
Looking light until nights begun
Firm footed stand of man's worth
Firm gaze until days undone.

Knight of light's end bound in white
While well wondered is western wind
Bearing in its arms those who've sinned
Bring darkness down that gleams still bright
Bring a devil as he laughed and grinned
At men that fight old chivalry's dying fight.

King undone in death's cold nights
Life's begun in Fate's living loom
And light within purest womb
Flesh feel what west wind bites
When innocent bound by in tomb
And first stars guide the dying light.

# Winter's Disposition

*Snow bowed bows bend loud in the quiet veil*
*Above, the winter burdened sky stoops low and pale*
*And leaves a cloudy kiss on the white clothed hill*
*Life stands still,*
*As white wind the air does fill*
*About the naked shoulders of the sleeping trees*
*Are white mantles laid by the gently biting breeze.*

*Foretold at the leaving of the living leaves*
*All the world stops, and no longer breathes*
*While whitened world lies wrapped is sleeping*
*Winds come sweeping,*
*Snow falls leaping*
*Frozen tears for lost warmth the skies weep*
*And the binding chills round the hills creep.*

*World is ice bound, hounded by the northwest*
*This world needs warm men with fire in their chest*
*The frost the earth a beauty's hardship does render*
*Burnt out ember*
*No one will remember*
*Winter's disposition cold hearts colder makes*
*And man's cold confidence it surly shakes.*

# St. Matthew's Passion

## Part I: The Last Supper - Arrest

*Hunger hangs on every man's lip*
*Gnawing at the souls with serpent's tooth*
*Thirsting for one more lying sip*
*Drinking bloody God's chaliced truth*
*Sustaining bread daily laid upon the table*
*Stone rejected is laid in the corner stable*

*Manna made fulfilled by opened hand*
*Last bread, first bread, breaded is the Word*
*Broken loaf, laid tombed in living land*
*Enter envy there to heat hearts having heard*
*Blessed breaking, raising saying "Take and eat"*
*Bread born by death treading, death dying feet*

*Drink and by death die no more*
*Covenant convert, and drink we you*
*Relished sip revealed in last of war*
*Righteous drop, dripped from redeeming True*
*Fruit gathered from an unveiled Vine*
*Is pressed to rest renewing watered wine*

*Taking bread by bowl betrayed*
*For a fallow field was our salvation sold*
*For trusting treason satisfaction never paid*
*And traitor's flesh hanging crimson cold*
*Silence hangs, within the calling world-cry*
*World waits while silver paid, silver to die*

*Sleep prayer of the falling flock sheep*
*First blood spilled by sweat of God's brow*
*While beyond kneels the bent headed God's weep*
*Soul-wrung Son praying for cup's pass now*
*Ringed round about by wolves of silver fleece*
*Traitor's kiss for a hell-hurled silver piece*

*Strike, the hearer's ear that he may hear more still*
*But meek soul is earth-heir and words fulfill*
*And willingly is debt paid at God's will*


## PART II: TRIAL – CROWNING OF THORNS

*False witness fails witness and ends*
*Following serpent's twin tongue smile*
*But in envy's twisted trial truth bends*
*But Divine will not answer man's mad trial*
*Even Rock lies shaking in lying's lair*
*And cock crows that Rock beware*

*Seated above the God sits reigning Rome*
*Asking justice for an Emperor and senate's sake*
*To now loving poisoned arms prisoner returning home*
*And bloody waters bloody hands bloodier make*
*They know not what they ask, the death of God*
*They ask again by Aron's full flower ringed rod*

*Blood lines for David's blood line*
*Whip sings stung song of crashing crown*
*Lashing lasts past sinning world, past time*
*Draw blood for Jacob's crown past down*
*Red flecked fallen dust of a fatal world*

Numbered bones not broken by the blows hurled
Whip's deviled rips flicks and flesh licks till red
God's blood mixed in blood of thieves that came before
Though heart scream for mercy's mean no word's said
Life beyond bounds of man's fragile bindings bore
Wombed to whips of men sin stained to bare
And crowns crashing whips with forgiving stare

Crowned King of Afflictions by insistent thorn
Stripped and struck, robed red as the dying sun
Spitted curses by the pagan pantheon sworn
Silent sits the throne in dust till path's begun
Thorned thousand for men's souls to death lost
Blows amount counted to pay man indebted cost

Accused, accursed, beaten and bone worn
Heaven's highest King honored by scorn
The first of his hallowed stainless flesh torn


## PART III: THE CARRYING OF THE CROSS – THE TOMB

Four sword now cut flesh in Virgin chest
First steps to first steps of cross bearing King
Looking longing to final breaths renewing rest
But slow and slow and slow steps to dust cling
Winding way longer made by life not yet shed
Limping lamb to the slaughter halter led

Forced charity's helping, lifting hand
Rising not Risen from dust clasped embrace
And on and up the jagged jut of dying's land
View unveiled of cross's hanging place

*Place of the skull where Adam's bone buried lies*
*Last steps to lay cross-ways and watch the skies*

*Lasting cries, and wine mixed gall*
*Cold iron pressed past hands, feet fastened fix crossed*
*Paying every soul from man's first fall*
*Lifted Light aloft, raising man's light lost*
*Casting die, below beleaguered bowing head*
*Cutting cloth that's stained from white to red*

*Breathe, take breath to breathe*
*Inspired, and inspirited, ghost gasp*
*Counting breaths till slip of soul's leave*
*With golden lips latched and key clasp*
*Waiting winged soul held in flesh fail*
*Transfixed fire, fixed by a cold calm nail*

*Fifth sword stabbing while hell-guarded ground shakes*
*Temple's vestment torn and lost Law rending rips*
*Calling "Elijah," elation's sorrow and soul walking wakes*
*Gates unguarded as thorn crowned head bending dips*
*Sixth sword maiden mother's harrowed heart harms*
*As Son immortal dead is laid within her virgin arms*

*Seven swords now driven in heart blessing bound*
*And tomb shut on a shrouded silent sound*
*Buried low, laid to rest beneath the ground*

# ON DRUNKENNESS

*I say be drunk and in drunkenness love*
*Sweet are the graces fallen from above*
*For in drunkenness man may find again his awe*
*And see again wonders that the ancients saw.*

*Sober, black and white follow rank on rank*
*Without love of God for which love we thank*
*False temperance, false piety man may gain*
*But with grace and wine man speaks Love's name.*

*To raise us up to God gave both grace and wine*
*To drink of love beauty and poetry's sweet line*
*Drunk on grace and Love's tender kisses*
*Before the beauty of the world man misses.*

*With grace and drunkenness we fill our days*
*And to heaven shall we go to be drunk always.*

# LONG FACES

*Long knight so with a long face*
*Lifted light and to a lifted place*
*Weakened heart in a clear glass case*
*Shattered window covered in softest lace*
*Bowed head from reason's reasoned chase*
*Shaking hand from a too long run race*

*Faced about in a sickening strict hallway*
*Strung and hung on a shaking born away*
*Buried down in the half shoveled clay*
*Covering lost light at the end of earth's day*
*Knees and tears falling down here to pray*
*God above for one night more to stay.*

# MOZART

*Rolling writhe of surging sound*
*Resound, reflect, regather in man*
*Cords' echos wrapped right round*
*Dwindling, down from a crashing grand.*

*Hold return to your quiet calm*
*Silence within the calling world-cry*
*Within a thousand tones of bathing balm*
*Quiet locked low no more to sigh.*

*Lie still o' man of the world*
*Rest your mind beyond the wind*
*Before your soul to hell hurled*
*Remember redeemed your soul sinned.*

*Wait before the rise of wrath*
*Braced before the quiet's cool embrace*
*But not look back on twice tread path*
*And know the roaring of the silent place*

.

# BEETHOVEN

*Or' pour my darkened chalice*
*Both dwindling dark and rising light*
*With but more than a glimpse of malice*
*Full fill the cup of limit, my sight.*

*Held gleaming on the ringing rim*
*My cup of life lent drunk low*
*Refill rising up on sweetest dim*
*Raging up peak path, but slow.*

*Then stop, step back away*
*To see the emptiness of half*
*See where is lacking, and pray*
*Pray Apollo for a lighted path.*

*The rising come with me on*
*Above the down dragging of the clay*
*Renew again lost light gone*
*Rising up to the newness of day.*

# Morning

Sunrise on your sleeping eyes
Wake with me and in waking walk
Breathe the spirit in your measure sighs
For sun we pray and do we ever talk.

Surety of sunrise are we never owed
No debt of light to us must be paid
Despite the proof that time has showed
No promised allotment to us is made.

Yet by faith or purest prayer
The sun will rise and touch below
To light a world still breathing air
The time will bring not fast not slow.

And light you as want and ought
And in your waking eyes is caught
Mirrored in flesh and wholesome thought
Given us, those who've never sought.

# FALSE HOPE

*When sunlight strikes upon a window sill*
*I feel the draw of warm wind and the hill*
*I hear streams falling cross stony bed*
*And spring time's songs fill up my head.*

*Cast off the aged sleep of winter's snow*
*To fields of life's muddy spring we'll go*
*For plowing planting and a new cycle grow*
*Then will that warm wind wash both high and low.*

*Spring's hope's sprung in my winter worn chest*
*Hope that again we may strive for what's best*
*Yet on looking out the snow wraps all*
*Winter's just begun its promise of new snow fall.*

*Frost's cold grip holds still the world as slave*
*And I snow bound, tombed within this cave.*

# THE CULTURE OF DEATH

White hands on themselves fall and rise
White faces with hollow staring eyes
Black curtains that block out every ray
Black thoughts that rather night than day.

Hollow beats on a hollow drum
They drum that night will never come
Hollow beats marked out by hollow hand
They say "never may we stop, never stand."

Virtue is no virtue in the places we have been
And sunlight hold no value in the places made for sin
The darkest night never dark enough for the shame of
their sin
Twice shadowed are the places we have been.

A shallow is all they've ever made
And sickly hearts adorned with diamond brocade
Second death in a half lived life inherited
No sin is owned no and no life is merited.

Lost in a sea of warm darkness's infections
And to self and outer self turns their affections
Not the noble death of the kings of old
Not a peaceful death, but blank and cold.

*Hell's dogs, black and fiery, panting Fury's foam*
*Sin sits in a corner closet, left unknown*
*As Pilate washed his hands, so the world is clean*
*Self justifies self, and everything does nothing mean.*

*Let Temptation lead temptation*
*Leave there no room for damnation*
*Let Temptation heal temptation*
*Leave there no room for salvation.*

*Forgotten fires of love and hate*
*Nature's salve has come, come too late*
*Forgotten fires of heaven and hell*
*All men bound by a saccharine satin spell.*

*Remember man that you are dust*
*And unto dust you shall return again*
*In our own hands is our life thrust*
*But there is no dust in the places we have been.*

# TO ART

*Restless are the hearts of men on earth*
*Until they die they search from their birth*
*For that lost thing to make us most content*
*Until man's mind is twisted and is bent.*

*They buy and take and everything spend*
*Not by pleasures or the gifts we lend*
*Are men happy, are men satisfied*
*Contentment we lost when Adam's purity died.*

*What can we do again to ease our mind?*
*But by art man his peace may find*
*As God created so now we may too*
*With hands, and heart we make and do.*

*Then man is most alive when he then bends his soul to art*
*Then body, mind and spirit beat, one heart.*

# THE BELLS

*The bells, the bells, what softest sound*
*Rolling out like water over parched ground*
*Splashing up and fall out of the sky*
*Droplets of sound unseen by the eye.*

*Or maybe like fire bursting into life*
*Kindled by man, the cause of all strife*
*With clashing, roaring bells burn up the sky*
*Bright sparks of sound unseen by the eye.*

*At that sound bright angels may take flight*
*Or wicked demons fly by darkest night*
*The cry of distress at wars begun*
*And up swords the fight is over and done.*

*For good and evil the bells both toll*
*And mark as time and history unroll.*

# THE WAR OF NIGHT AND DAY

*Now Night has fallen that he might slay the Sun*
*His wind-sung sword held with strength in hand*
*May all weaker light before him flee and run*
*Before him none may fight or make a stand.*

*When Darkness creeps with teeth and sneering lip*
*Behind they come, Light's blood on their daggers still*
*And from the poisoned cup they ask you sip*
*In Night's hoard they march with panting thirst to kill.*

*Daylight lies west and bleeds out on the ground*
*Legion stands in rank behind death gifting Night*
*The war is lost and we are chained and bound*
*All the world groans under Death's crushing might.*

*"The stars," cries the out all the conquered earth*
*With hope for light, for love, and sweet rebirth*
*All bow to the Virgin Moon, mantled all in white*
*Veiled in purity of jeweled justice's light.*

*Great is the strength of ten thousand stars*
*Pouring down on windy steeds from heavens far*
*At godlike Jupiter's command and Moon's sweet prayer*
*They wheel and charge, the forbidding Night they dare.*

*The greatest knights Sirius, Arcturus, and Leo*
*And their shining soldiers in time held maneuvers go*
*The waring twins, Gemini's most holy rage*
*Cut the sky from where they've sat from first age.*

And from the might halls of Mount Alberion
The spears of a thousand lights march, march on
They come singing hope to all the enslaved earth
They come singing all to renew man's broken worth

As cohorts of shrouded demons turn and face
The mighty Taurus, his lightning strength felt in every place
Everywhere across the subdued world the war is seen
As unearthly forces war as war has never been.

They clash and turn across the Night ruled sky
Their lighted blood is spilt that man no more may die
Night howling for Day's destruction and his kingdom
While Moon looks on, silent in her quiet wisdom.

Fires burn across the war racked ranks
And Darkness pressed up against the western banks
Fires of sin and deadly Death and still fight on
But within each heart there rests the hope for the coming Dawn

Then before the cunning Night may know
The Sun is risen and strikes all with grace's glow
Thrown down upon the ground is Darkness, Night has fled
And cleansing waters quench Death's fire, Death is dead.

All the broken world breathes again anew
As Sun, Daylight, and Warm Wind the ruler true
Take again the Throne and light the new-born
World.  Now is time to build and mend what war has torn.

All is bright, all is just and mercy reigns
Warmth and a new blood runs within man's veins
And still the stars stand guard in heavens above.
While Moon prays at the King's throne of love.

# With Dante

The King of kings with his omnipotent might
Seemed to me to be but a far off light.
As a star cold and distant, sees the world that's His
And on a throne of justice judges all that is

And I but the humblest peasant in his kingdom
Am but a tool in the hand of His wisdom
Which when broken is to be cast away
Night comes quickly when sin rules the way.

Far off I see the mountain rise from the start
But lost in the darkness I lost my heart
Then comes Dante with the humble torch of poetry
And leads the road marked clear by the Tree.

There stands the Son with the eyes of man
With mercy and grace in either hand.

# THE EYES OF THE BELOVED

*Like some ancient sailor far out at sea*
*Around him all are waves and wind and he*
*Yet far off is fixed the stars by which he sails*
*so your eyes are fixed guide when my word fails.*

*Outside is darkness all around the door*
*A window in the night can light all the more*
*By such transparency is inside seen*
*So your eyes show what heart does mean.*

*Far off the sun's light seems to lie*
*And I have not the wings to upward fly*
*But sapphired mirrors are your eyes to me*
*Reflecting light that I might see.*

*Your eyes' mirrors show me, lead me God's holy light*
*Of love and light mirrored in eyes blue bright.*

# TEMPTATION

I rage in battle's frenzied surge
I clash with foes that flank my every side
All I can do to burn and poison purge
No place there is to run or hide.

Virtue's sword is chipped and even broken
The metal's weak that guards my embattled heart
And twisted are the words I've already spoken
And warring souls threaten to tear apart.

Upon shaking legs I face my enemy
One more time they turn and climbing come
I know my falling is near, but must it be
Instead I turn and cut and run

To my Lady's blue, white warming embrace
Safe from falling's danger I do race.

# KNOWLEDGE'S PATHS

*How is man to learn to reach the heavens' height*
*What road to take to find eternal light*
*Should he by pen and dead bound book be learned*
*Or with the world reach what its man has yearned.*

*With turning page and endless written words*
*He'll learn of a far off God that justice girds*
*All creation that's Maker's face is in his mind*
*He needs not eyes, for all he could be blind.*

*But tree, and stone and heaven's flying bird*
*To hold and see what's done in Maker's Word*
*No book man need see what is all God's face*
*For His heart it is that beats in every place*

*Then live in this full world that He has made*
*To know that Love no teacher need be paid.*

# CHOICES

*The choice is mine to run or should I stand?*
*It is this way that all men live, in choice*
*To take the road or die with plow in hand*
*To walk in quiet or sing with joyful voice.*

*At every point the paths that are diverge*
*To walk the world or work the blessed land*
*I'll sing with joy or live my doleful dirge*
*To die in comfort or on some lonesome strand.*

*If as a bird I had ability*
*I'd build my nest take again to flight*
*With both my freedom and stability*
*And life's burdens and it toils become then light*

*But I am man and so must choose*
*Which road I'll take, which path I'll use.*

# THE DOORS

On warm evenings we'd walk the street
Walked we then on too sure of feet
Warmed by whiskey, love, and pavement's heat
And pass the crowed people behind open doors.

We'd sit a while on the banks of the river
Cool wind from out north would make us shiver
Given kisses both the given and the giver
And though we're cold we'd rather not go indoors.

Old men sit in a doorway's bending arch
Young men step in time and aging march
While the women whisper gossip's words under leaning larch
The house is locked by the windows and the doors.

On a cool gray morning to St. Benedict's we'd go
The doors open and shut as the cockles grow
And the shrouded sun burns with a pale glow
After, Church stands empty, but with open doors.

The door that shut when man first fell
Opened all the doors that open hell
These dark doors do men know too well
Now all is open wide, all look you to the doors.

# DEATH IS NOT YOUR MASTER

Death is not your master, and you are not his slave,
For you were made a free man
When you were just a babe.

A: Darkness rest upon your young head
    You do not sleep in your healing bed
    Haunted by some wrong word you've read
    Resting on thoughts of men not yet dead

B: Well laid is the foundation of my life
    But all my tools are broken, every hammer, every
    knife

A: Well made is the steel that is your very heart
    And yet you think that you are torn apart

B: Some shelter from the winds raw strength
    I ask of you and yours for the shortest length

A: You've made yourself a beggar, made yourself blind
    But still come in and put things from your mind

Death is not your master, and you are not his slave.
For you were born a free man
When he laid within the grave.

# The Mask

Masks are for thieves, walking in the night
Laying their hand on whatever they may find
Hiding from justice, and virtue's light
They wear masks to hide the face and mind.

Masks are for actors saying to please
In motion and in speech they do seem
To hold their virtue with saint's subtle ease
But hiding their vices, virtue's mask does gleam.

I'll wear no mask nor hide myself
My virtues and my vices I will plainly
I'll not put my sins away to fester on a closet shelf
But live unhidden though I'm strong, though weak

In a mask lies greater vice than vice alone
A vicious pride that rot man to his bone.

# THE GLORY OF DEATH

When at the close of day the sun grows old
And darkness rise to meet the fading light
The sun it strains and show all strength she holds
She paints the sky in colors clear and bright.

The wounded horse that faces his last breath
He fights with rage to match the pounding sea
None can his fury brave, his eyes are set on death
In his last hour meets his end with glory.

What strength and might in this frail world abide?
The tree the ax resists until the last
The highest point of sea's receding tide
The sparrow with its beating heart so fast.

The worth of things is hid until the end
Then truth and might come clear with sickle's bend.

# BEFORE THE WORLD WAS COLD

*The men of the days we call old*
*Before the world had become cold*
*They and their virtues were than bold*
*Before the world's beauty was ever sold*
*Then did men wisdom and piety hold*
*And man knew the Word that God had told*
*He looked up and watched the skies unfold*
*God with his starry hand man did mold*
*And charity was man's treasured gold.*

*Then in mountain halls so near the sky*
*Did men aid the world as it went by*
*To follow the Word man need not try*
*Then did man work and not die*
*And with the lion did his children lie*
*Man saw with the birds as they'd fly*
*Never a tear fell down from his eye*
*And man sat on the world's throne high*
*That throne is lost and no men ask why.*

*Now it is the close of day*
*The sun counts her every ray*
*And the devil counts the souls that pay*
*Man's lover, Charity on tender feet flees away*
*And on graves of fallen foe children play*
*While the strong man looses what his power may*
*Now God gathers the world back to clay.*

# MARK THE MUSIC 1

Mark the music, how it rises and falls
Notes souls lift, notes soul's gift
And hearts as a tender lover calls,
Where before was chasm and rift
And depression's disposition music may yet shift.

Of man music expounds when logics fail
Beneath man's eye, beneath man's cry
Melody is found that alone can lift his veil
At soul's roots music's strings do lie
That when played well man may not die.

Man's grown deaf though the music's not broken
Man's soul paid, man's soul made
By harmonies the Word has always spoken
Though our hearts in our falling fade
Musics still stand holding out man's aid.

The foundations of the world laid on this strength
This world's bind, this world's mind
Is made of music of eternal length
When this world ends we may yet find
Music everlasting, music of God's kind.

# THE ROADSIDE

*The roadside's ridden with wayward wanderings*
*Broken, beset, and battered are the wings*
*That bear you like some god's hand*
*And at the roadside bound by broken bands.*

*Whispering wandering in your deafened ear*
*Words wasted on misapprehensions and fear*
*While wastrel eyes on a crucifix look*
*Lost lies first poetry, and that first book.*

*Undefended though defeated are those wider ways*
*Away the mean measured for all man's days*
*No better the meaningless miles of their roadside*
*There are no words that they to you confide.*

*While others battle by on narrow roads beyond*
*There's none that love the roadside or found fond*
*Injured without fighting, for them no bell rings*
*Blank eyes, bland minds have wasted wanderings.*

# Your Light (To a lover)

*Not distant like the stars in their old places*
*Not like the sickly light of moon's face's*
*And overwhelming is the scorching of the sun*
*Your light can be compared this way to none.*

*Instead is warm and bright without such pain*
*And with the days it does not wax or wane*
*The eye can see but mouth enough not tell*
*Not words, but verse alone become you well.*

*Your light beside you stands and will not sink*
*As flames within a fire wither and shrink*
*Of your light's cup I'd only ask a drink*
*For light there is that man not have to think.*

*You look and cast your undiminished light*
*Your light it burns, and burning grows more bright.*

# THE DISCUSSION

*I have no use for poets or poetry. They play too*
*fast and loose with grammar's rules. To talk around*
*the point's no good to me. The words are flattery that*
*ought to be a tool. They must be backwards in their aged*
*notions. To cling to used up words of love and death, and*
*think that this world moves in music's motions. I see but*
*vanity, it's all a waste of breath.*

*Your own words betray you now*
*For as poetry you so disclaim*
*You speak as you know not how*
*In metered, rhythm curse poetry's name.*

*The world is poetry through and through,*
*The tallest mountain down to the smallest stone*
*Sing in verse, yes and even you*
*Held as whole your blood and your bone.*

*Beauty you can't escape or truth evade*
*We eat it breathe it and make it ours*
*And without poetry is nothing ever made*
*We are all poets born, unto our last hour.*

# I Saw My Love Go Walking

I saw my love go walking, walking in the sunset
I heard my love come singing, singing soft and low
Her song was sad and lonesome and filled up with regret.
She walked out towards the west where I could not go.
I stood far off and listened there until her song was done,
She sighed and bowed her head beneath the bloody sun.

"The men I've loved don't know me now," were the words she
sang.
"I gave them life I gave them love and still they look away."
Her words they fell and as a bell softly so they rang
"My time is done, and I will go just as the close of day."
I knew her pain, I felt her loss deep within my chest,
And stood there lonely as she slipped away, away off to the
west.

The sun went down and night's cold cloak spread out still and
wide
Alone I walked in wind and dark, there without a light
"Where to go?" I asked myself and looked from side to side
And threw me down in deep despair to fade into the night.
There I lay but then looked up, and saw the stars above
Within their light I found my hope for there I saw my love.

# HOMER'S BROAD DOMAIN

*My love is in the wind, she's blown away from me*
*On soft shod feet she walks in mountains that were lost*
*When man gave up his gifted share of poetry,*
*When man cast off his crown and rivers ancient crossed.*
*This land he forfeit,this ungrateful heir,*
*And hidden is she now in golden kingdoms there.*

*My love is in a rooftop garden that looks out on the sea*
*Where ships come to and sail away with holds of*
*        treasured verse*
*And stories of a place afar so few may ever see*
*The port is quiet now, its memr'y men now curse*
*And still my love she stand and looks out to the sea*
*In that lost land she stands and waits for me.*

*On that rooftop I once stood and held my love's hand*
*From there we looked across the land and saw the hill*
*Where Homer's crowned citadel under golden cornice stand*
*And muses dance with Venus where the streams sings still*
*But I have left and gone my darkened plodding way*
*With but a hope that I would yet return to her one day/*

*Twice I'd pay and sell my life away*
*For my love's kiss, and one last day*
*Upon those shore that man may never sway.*

# If I Loved Her

She stands there a solitary figure
As plain as any other who stops
And turns her face up to the light
To feel the warmth and see the sky.

How would I see her standing there
If she were framed by my affections
If she were not a stranger to my care
If saw her in the light of love's projections.

She would stand there still yet aflame
With a ringing beauty as a gilded bell
A light with love that shadow never shame
As if on her the light of heavens far off fell.

Beneath her graceful glancing feet
The grass not bend but bow and lie
And sing when they and she in passing meet
Happy for her beauty just to pass them by.

From her would waft a breeze of grace
Both warm and cool the succure of my soul
Before her stands there none, none that could replace
A healing beauty here to make me whole.

Let all such visions pass and fade
For she is not so, she is no light
Though only by my lack she lack
Such beauty and such grace.

# Hymn 1

*Oh my Lord open my eyes / give me light and let me see*
*My soul is dark, my heart is hidden / My face is turned away*
*I have spent my nights in sleeplessness / I have washed my face in tears*
*I see not the coming morning / or the stars in their brightness*
*I have cast myself down on the earth / I have turned my face from the heavens*
*The leopard stalks me in the darkness / He finds me lost on the mountain*
*The lion lies in wait for me / He hunts me in the valley*
*The wolf stands and guards the pass / She rises to there to block my way*
*Oh my Lord lend me your protection / Put your sword into my hand*
*A sword of grace and light / To guard me from my afflictions*
*Yet my hand shakes when I wield it / I cannot deal a mortal wound*
*Oh my Lord where is your shield / Why have you forsaken me*
*Have I not stood upright in your eyes / And spoke your name with love*
*Have I not followed the path you set / Unquestioning I have walked*
*The way is lost and all have turned against me / I am forsaken to my enemies*

*The fortress of my heart is well defended / Yet my enemies lie within the walls*
*Men love the downfall of the righteous / They take joy in their iniquity*
*All I have accomplished has come undone / I have done my works in vain*
*I have stored up grain and wine / But the Deceiver came and whispered to me*
*I sold him all that I owned / He left me empty handed*
*Now my fields are harvested / But all my barns are empty.*

# HYMN 2

*I have stilled my soul like the night / Like a cool and windless night so is my soul*
*Your voice is like a cooling water / My heart is dry and bears no fruit*
*I have cried to you in my affliction / Why then do you not answer me*
*I wait for answer in the darkness / Like dew in the night you come to men*
*Why then do I labor under the sun / When you give to your beloved in their sleep*
*Gifts are given to those who asked / More is given to those who wait in silence*
*In the silence of my soul you will speak / In the darkness you are seen*
*I speak not words of wisdom / I have humbled my heart before you*
*My eyes are not raised too high above me / I do not seek vain glory*
*My foes rage about the fortress / Yet I sit quiet within the walls*
*The walls of my Lord were build with strength / Against them no force of men may prevail.*

# THE RIVER GOD

*This was no Scamander, who fought the great Achilles*
*Who in his wrath he churned and surged and rapids raged*
*He was but a young one by the old gods' count*
*Filled with laughing at the playful minds of men*
*Singing along his banks for the lovers that came to him*
*And told him all their love, and their desires*
*And their dreams, their dreams.*

*He was born up in the mountains' heights where sky and*
*        earth collide*
*The mountain nymph that bore him was the lover of the sea*
*Since then it has been not long by the old gods' count*
*Since when he first lept lightly down the mountain slopes*
*        in spring*
*To sing with man his love and life and all he ever knew*
*And there dreams, there dreams*

*But he has gone away now, this younger river god.*
*Gone somewhere southward, returning to the sea.*
*No more to be seen sleek within his banks, or*
*Singing with the souls of men, to tell them what he knows*
*For men no longer ask him, no longer do they sing*
*And he has gone away now to his father in the sea*
*And there dreams, there dreams*

# Now

*A warm slide of my cigarette, and out slips*
*Smoke wreathed beauty before the close of day*
*Bitter of coffee against sweetness of Love's lips*
*I turn you and you turn to me, love's name to say.*

*Hand-taking takes mind and breaks time*
*A wedging moment between the future and the past*
*Watching the sun lean west behind you, mine.*
*Talk to me between next moment and the last.*

*Time winds onward while we sit near*
*Bright eyes in a dying lighted world*
*The moment wavers and then comes clear*
*Blue smoke around our eyesights' climbing curled.*

*Time lost is love lost in hourglass dunes*
*Careless heart carefully tossed before your feet*
*Lips sing brings notes of love's lilting tunes*
*To bearing's edge our souls driven by mind's meet.*

*These are the days we will remember*
*When worn warm flesh burns an ember*
*Hold this 'now' as 'now' before memory's tripped*
*'Now' wings west and by holding held is slipped.*

# THE WIND

Whipped whispers winding on the breeze
Falling sighing through the bent blown trees
Thrown skyward and thrash down on bended knees
Cold fangs of a newborn beast holding heaven's keys.

Breathe as the broken sky screaming dies
Lashed cross the land leviathan lies
Writhe unridden sinewed straining rise
Drive me wrecked, and striving up-flies.

Heaven wracked stars flee faster than the sun
Hear the billow, the roar of heaven's heavy gun
Swift slip sounded in the night before light's come
Drift drip drownded in the dark before night's done.

Windswept stars born headlong high, away
By the unseen frenzied force foaming spray
Before Aeolus all the world does shrink and sway
Begging gods for the breaking of a softer day.

Off and down the wild wind swept hills
Between the battered trees of forest fills
And wrap the candle round till flame kills
While through the window winged ghost shrills.

Rising to a leaf riding steed... and slow
Slow, slipping sideways but always low
Silent dripping winding leaves below
Stillness born of wind-song's ceasing blow.

# I Felt a Motion

*I felt a motion low in my soul*
*Somewhere beneath the mind*
*Behind my heart in my chest*
*A longing a yearning for light*
*And a hatred for all things false.*

*They called the car but I declined*
*Saying I needed some cool night air*
*I'd walk I said though why I don't know*
*Why did I walk when I could just drive*
*The wind was moaning soft behind me*
*On nights such as these each man is alone.*

*Somewhere, away up the hill*
*In the swarming darkness the bell rung*
*It fell, hung, and darkness knell wrung*
*The sound of held hope wafting down the hills*
*Still the darkness swept around me*
*With the whispered wind*
*Dark enough that any man would go blind, but*
*From the mouth of that blind poet we will see*
*Tiresias looks on with tears*
*Dripping from his unseeing eyes*
*I turn right seeing a light before me, but*
*Stumbled, when I rose I found*
*I had always faced left, and that light left.*

On this same night as I stumbled through the darkness
The scholar bent low over his book
By him the stub of a candle burned
Low.  Such a light, so high in ivory, so low
Seemed cold and watery weak to me
Where I lay on the earth below, his tower
So speaks Tiresias:
"They shall draw their swords against you
And the beauty of your Wisdom."

I have looked around me
I gave names to the cattle
And the birds of the air
And all things that walk, or crawl, or fly
And the dappled-with-damson sky
All things dappled, distinctive, and bright
All these were given me to be mine
And yet I lack
For nowhere could I find in this garden
Bone of my bone, flesh of my flesh
Nowhere a fit companion.

To the South stands Aphrodite smiling fragrantly
In the North bright eyed Athena beckons
Hera stands to the East a knot in her hand
But I will go out West still searching, searching
Where oh Beatrice are you walking.

www.ingramcontent.com/pod-product-compliance
Lightning Source LLC
Chambersburg PA
CBHW021940040426
42448CB00008B/1159